THE NATIONAL TRUST
*Little Library*

# *Ice & Creams*
## SORBETS

JILL NORMAN

DORLING KINDERSLEY
LONDON

## A DORLING KINDERSLEY BOOK

EDITOR  LAURA HARPER

SENIOR EDITOR  CAROLYN RYDEN

DESIGN  MATHEWSON BULL

PHOTOGRAPHER  DAVE KING

FIRST PUBLISHED IN GREAT BRITAIN IN 1990 BY
DORLING KINDERSLEY LIMITED
9 HENRIETTA STREET, LONDON WC2E 8PS

BRITISH LIBRARY CATALOGUING IN PUBLICATION DATA

NORMAN, JILL
ICE CREAMS & SORBETS
I. ICE CREAMS – RECIPES
I. TITLE II. SERIES
641·863

ISBN 0-86318-491-X

PRINTED AND BOUND IN HONG KONG
BY IMAGO

# CONTENTS

# INTRODUCTION

*19th-century ice breaker*

*T*HE CHINESE *used ice to conserve food as long ago as 1100BC, and built ice houses to store winter ice through the summer. The Roman emperors, in their turn, had snow brought from the Alps to cool their wine, and conserved it under thick straw mats. The Mogul rulers of India had ice and snow brought to Delhi from the Himalayas. Travellers in 16th-century Turkey wrote of vaults packed with the snow and ice used to dilute sherbets (fruit drinks). At the Sultan's court bowls for dessert were fashioned out of frozen fruit juice.*

*The Italians seem to have invented what we would call ices, and artificial freezing started there in the early 17th century. Cream was scalded, sweetened and flavoured with puréed fruit or jam, then put in tin ice pots which were immersed in buckets lined with straw and filled with ice, salt and saltpetre.*

*By the middle of the century ices had spread to the court at Versailles and from there to the other courts of Europe. They were expensive commodities and did not become widely available until the end of the century when eaux glacées and neiges were made by the guild of* limonadiers *and sold in the fashionable cafés of Paris.*

*In England ice houses were built on country estates and ice cream making followed. The English gained their first knowledge of making ices from translations of French books. The earliest English recipe appears in* Mrs Eales' Recipes, *1718. In 1751 Hannah Glasse added ices (stirred as they were frozen in pewter basins) to her book*

*The Art of Cookery Made Plain and Easy. Later books had elaborate recipes for frozen mousses, iced creams and water ices. The French kept to water ices – a pattern that persisted. Mixtures were now frozen in moulds called* sarbotières, *which were turned until the contents were frozen. Ices intended for decorative moulds, which were much in vogue, were started in a* sarbotière *and transferred to the mould set in ice and salt.*

*Ice creams, rather than water ices, became fashionable in the United States towards the end of the 18th century. George Washington had an ice machine, and Jefferson served* omelette surprise *(baked Alaska). But until the invention of the crank freezer in 1846 ices remained hard to make. Then sales boomed and America was set to become the ice cream leader of the world.*

*Today ices are enjoyed the world over. There seems almost no limit to the ingredients that taste good in frozen form; I hope this little book encourages you to experiment with making ices at home.*

*19th-century ice cream street seller*

# SOFT FRUIT
# ICE CREAMS &
# SORBETS

*T*HERE ARE TWO *main varieties of ices:*
*water ice is made of a water-and-sugar syrup*
*with a flavouring, usually fruit;* **ice cream** *has a cream base,*
*or an egg yolk-and-cream custard for a richer*
*and smoother result. Sorbet (or sherbet) is a*
*smooth-textured water ice to which beaten egg*
*whites have been added; granita is a water ice*
*in which the coarse texture of large ice*
*crystals is preserved.*
*Ripe soft fruits make*
*intensely flavoured*
*ices and sorbets.*

*Blackberries*

*Raspberries*

Strawberries

Raspberry
ripple
ice cream

Red currants

Wild
strawberries

Blackberry
ice cream

Blackcurrants

Strawberry
ice cream

# CITRUS & STONE FRUIT ICES

*M*AKING ICED DESSERTS *at home gives absolute control over ingredients and a fresher, tastier result. Water ices do not need special equipment, they can be frozen in a shallow tray as long as they are stirred thoroughly once or twice, but a small ice cream machine that simultaneously churns and freezes will give a smoother result.*

Lemon and orange water ices are the easiest basic ices to make at home, and as with all fresh fruit ices their flavour is far more intense and 'natural' than that of any bought variety. Hollow the skins and fill them with the ice for an unusual dessert.

*Lemon sorbet*

*Orange*

*Plum*

Orange sorbet

Lemon

Nectarine

Peach

# EXOTIC FRUIT ICE
# CREAMS & SORBETS

*THE LIGHT, REFRESHING FLAVOURS of exotic
fruits are very successful in sorbets. All
sorbets 'should be of a light semi-frozen nature, having
only just sufficient consistency to hold together when piled
up. . . . They are generally prepared by first
making an ordinary lemon water ice, and
adding to this some spirit, liqueur, or syrup for
flavouring, and fruit for garnish. . . . They
are always served in cups or glasses.'*
Agnes Marshall,
The Book of
Ices, *1885.*

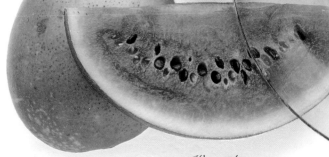

*Watermelon*

*Mango*

Pineapple

Watermelon
sorbet

Kiwi fruit

Pineapple
ice cream

Passion fruit

The delicate colours of
these fruits, further
softened by egg white,
contribute much to the
decorative effect.

# DRIED FRUIT &
# UNUSUAL ICES

*U*NUSUAL AND COLOURFUL ICES
*have always been popular. The Americans*
*have been the most inventive people in the commercial*
*history of ice cream. Ice cream sodas, for example, were*
*a huge success at the Centennial Exposition in Phila-*
*delphia in 1879. Novelties such as eskimo pie and ice*
*cream on a stick became fashionable in the Twenties;*
*more and more flavours were produced – many based on*
*synthetics – but today emphasis is on pure ingredients.*

*19th-century*
*ice cream maker*

Small pieces of dried fruit
provide contrast in texture
and colour, not only in tutti
frutti ice cream. On these
pages are raisins and
sultanas, citron peel (pale
green), candied orange
peel, angelica (green) and
glacé cherries.

*Tutti frutti
ice cream*

# NUT ICES

*Filippo Baldini, a Naples physician,
recommended pistachio and pine nut
sorbets as being good for the digestion
(De' Sorbetti, 1784 ). They were
made with milk obtained by soak-
ing crushed nuts in cold water and
pressing out the essence of the
nuts to give a cloudy milky
liquid. Almond milk is still
used in southern Italy to
make an excellent sorbet.
A similar process is fol-
lowed in pistachio ice
cream (p.36). Nuts now
flavour a variety of ices
from pecan to macadamia.*

*Pistachio
ice cream*

*Walnut*

*Pistachios*

*Almond*

Assorted
nuts

Walnut
ice cream

Almond
ice cream

15

# CHOCOLATE, TEA & COFFEE ICES

*C*HOCOLATE AND COFFEE *were used in Italy from an early date as flavouring for sorbets, and coffee granita (p.30), with its grainy texture and ice shards, is still the best ice for a hot day. Scented teas such as Earl Grey and jasmine make delicate sorbets and ices; the more robust flavours of chocolate and coffee combine well with nuts or alcohol for ice creams.*

*Grated chocolate*

*Chocolate ice cream*

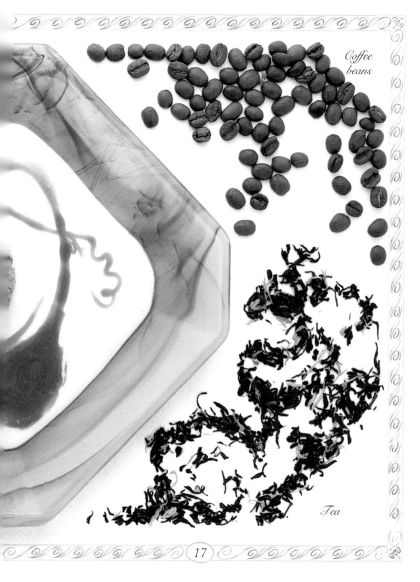

Coffee
beans

Tea

# SPICED ICES

*W*O LITTLE GIRLS OF TEN *and twelve years of age, pow-dered and tightly laced into their pointed bodices, sat facing a boy of about fifteen . . . and an old lady in black (certainly the governess) ; all were eating large ices of an odd pink colour, maybe of cinnamon, rising in sharp cones from long glass goblets.'* Lampedusa's description of a painting in his Sicilian home (Two Stories and a Memory, *trans. 1962*).

In India *kulfi* is flavoured with cardamom. The English have adopted preserved ginger for a rich after-dinner ice. Vanilla is probably the most widely used spice, and a custard-based ice made with a vanilla pod is hard to beat. For an even more intense flavour, scrape the seeds from the pod and leave them in the mixture.

*Ginger ice cream*

*Cardamoms*

*Mace & nutmeg*

Fresh ginger

Cinnamon
sticks

Chopped
ginger

Cinnamon
ice cream

Preserved
ginger

Ground cinnamon

Vanilla pod

# ICES WITH WINE & SPIRITS

*A*LCOHOL, *whether a straight spirit such as whisky or rum, or a liqueur such as cointreau or crème de cassis, is a useful flavouring for ice creams, but do not add too much or the mixture will not freeze. Champagne and sweet wines – Sauternes and muscats – make refreshing sorbets. In England the use of alcohol in ices comes under the licensing laws, which is why you cannot buy real rum and raisin from an ice cream shop.*

*Orange & cointreau ice cream*

*Rum*

*Whisky*

Rum & raisin
ice cream

Cassis
ice cream

Cassis

Cognac

Cointreau

# HONEY, SYRUP &
# SUGAR IN ICES

*S*WEETENING IS AS IMPORTANT *as flavour-ing in ice cream. It determines texture – if there is too little, the ice will be grainy; if there is too much, it will not freeze. Caster sugar in which a vanilla pod has been immersed is a good all-purpose sweetener for ices, and brown sugar, honey, maple syrup and caramel all have specific uses.*

*Selection of 19th-century moulds*

There is a special delight in the old-fashioned presentation of ices in the shaped moulds of which there used to be such infinite variety, mostly made of pewter. In their heyday ices from moulds provided decoration as well as amusement, such as sorbets disguised as the very glasses in which they might have been served.

*Soft brown sugar*

Maple syrup

Honey

Honeycomb

Acacia
honey
ice cream

Soft brown sugar

# Recipes

*All the recipes will serve 4*

## MAKING ICE CREAMS AND WATER ICES

The quickest method for making an ice is to mix a flavouring – fruit juice or purée; alcohol, coffee, tea; herbs or spices – with a syrup to make a water ice or with cream to make an ice cream.

The simplest water ice – a granita – is a thick, grainy slush. It can be refined by the addition of beaten egg white to make a sorbet. A basic ice cream of cream, sweetening and flavouring is light and delicate; ices with a richer texture and flavour are made with a custard of egg yolks and cream.

Most ice creams and sorbets taste best when eaten the day they are made. After a few days in the freezer many will have frozen so hard that they must be softened before serving, to bring out their flavour and improve their texture. Put them in the refrigerator for 10–30 minutes before serving, depending on the type of ice and the container in which it is stored.

## FREEZING METHODS

The most satisfactory method is to use one of the small domestic ice cream machines which freeze and churn simultaneously. Follow the manufacturer's instructions for use.

Ices can also be frozen in shallow trays. Set the freezer to its lowest setting before starting to make the ice. It will need beating once or twice during the freezing process to break up the large ice crystals which form.

When the mixture has set around the sides and on the bottom of the tray, tip it out into a chilled bowl and beat vigorously. Then return it to the tray and to the freezer.

## *B*ASIC SYRUP FOR SORBETS

*2 lb/1 kg sugar*
*1³/₄ pints/1 litre water*

Put the sugar and water into a heavy pan and bring slowly to the boil, stirring until the sugar has dissolved. Simmer for 5 minutes, then cool.
The syrup can be kept in a bottle in the refrigerator for up to a month.

# BLACKCURRANT SORBET

1 lb/500 g blackcurrants
3–4 tablespoons water
1/2 pint/300 ml syrup (p.25)
2 tablespoons crème de cassis
(optional)

Put the blackcurrants (there is no need to remove stalks) in a pan with a little water to prevent them sticking, and simmer until the juices run and the fruit is soft. Rub the fruit through a fine sieve and leave the purée to cool. Mix the purée with the syrup and cassis, and freeze.

# BLUEBERRY SORBET

1 1/2 lb/750 g blueberries
8–10 oz/250–300 g caster sugar
2 tablespoons crème de myrtilles or
1 tablespoon lemon juice

Purée the blueberries in a food processor and then sieve to ensure that the purée is smooth. Add the sugar and heat gently until it has dissolved. Cool, then stir in the crème de myrtilles or lemon juice and freeze.

# ELIZA ACTON'S RED CURRANT ICE

'Strip the stalks and take *two pounds weight of fine ripe currants* and *half a pound of raspberries*; rub them through a fine sieve, and mingle thoroughly with them sufficient cold syrup to render the mixture agreeably sweet, and, – unless the pure flavour of the fruit be altogether preferred, – add *the strained juice of one large or of two small lemons*, and proceed at once to freeze.

*Currants, 2 lbs; raspberries, 1/2 lb; sugar 3/4–1 lb; boiled for 6 or 8 minutes in 1/2 pint of water and left till quite cold. (Juice of lemon or lemons at pleasure.)*'

Eliza Acton, *Modern Cookery*, 1845

## Pomegranate Sorbet

*juice of 3 large pomegranates
(about ¹/₂ pint/300 ml)
¹/₂ pint/300 ml syrup (p.25)
zest of 1 orange
juice of 1 lemon
1 egg white*

Strain the pomegranate juice
and mix with the syrup, orange
zest and lemon juice. Whisk the
egg white until stiff and fold in
before freezing in an ice cream
machine, or once you have
obtained a thick slush if freezing
in trays (see p.28).

## Mango Sorbet

*3 ripe mangoes
¹/₂ pint/300 ml syrup (p.25)
juice of 1 lime*

Peel the mangoes and cut the
flesh from the stones. Purée the
fruit – you should have about
³/₄ pint/450 ml purée. Stir in the
syrup and lime juice and freeze.

# LEMON SORBET

*¹/₂ pint/300 ml lemon juice*
*zest of 3 lemons*
*³/₄ pint/450 ml syrup (p.25)*
*2 egg whites*

Combine the lemon juice, zest and syrup. If you are freezing the sorbet in a tray in the freezer, cover it and freeze for 2–3 hours, stirring occasionally, until you have a thick slush, then whisk the egg whites until stiff and fold in the ice mixture. Return to the freezer in a larger container and leave to freeze. If you use an ice cream machine, fold in the whisked egg whites before putting the mixture into the machine.

# FROSTED ORANGES

*4 large oranges*
*juice of 1 lemon*
*5 oz/150 g caster sugar*
*1 egg white*

Wash the oranges well and cut a lid from the top of each one. Scoop out the flesh with a small spoon and put the shells and lids in the freezer whilst you prepare the sorbet.

Put the fruit pulp in a juicer or food processor. Strain the juice, add the lemon juice and sugar, and stir to dissolve the sugar. Whisk the egg white until stiff, fold it into the mixture and freeze in an ice cream machine. If you are freezing the sorbet in trays, add the egg white when the mixture has set to a slush. Fill the orange shells when the mixture has almost set. Put on the lids and keep in the freezer. Frosted oranges are best served on the day they are made.

# CHAMPAGNE SORBET

The more robust the champagne, the better the sorbet. Other sparkling wines such as a crémant de Bourgogne or a sparkling Saumur can be used instead.

*6 oz/175 g sugar*
*juice of 2 oranges*
*juice of 1 lemon*
*3/4 pint/450 ml champagne*

Dissolve the sugar in the fruit juice and chill until very cold. Chill the champagne. Pour the champagne into the juice, pouring against the side of the container to prevent it frothing too much. Freeze and serve on the day it is made – it does not keep well.

## Variation

Make a champagne and strawberry sorbet with a purée made from 12 oz/350 g strawberries and a tablespoon of lemon juice instead of the orange and lemon juice.

# APPLE SORBET WITH CALVADOS

*3/4 pint/450 ml syrup (p.25)*
*5 tart green apples, cored and chopped*
*3 fl oz/75 ml calvados*

Heat the syrup and add the chopped apples. Simmer for 10–15 minutes, until the apples are soft, then leave to cool. When cold, purée the mixture, add the calvados and freeze.

# COFFEE GRANITA

The most refreshing ice for
a hot day.
*1¹/₄ pints / 750 ml very strong coffee*
*a strip of lemon rind*
*4 oz / 125 g caster sugar*
*whipped cream*

Infuse the lemon rind and
dissolve the sugar in the coffee.

Leave it to cool, then remove the
lemon rind and freeze the
mixture in trays, stirring every
30 minutes until you have a
thick granular slush. Serve in
tall glasses, topped with
whipped cream.

# _F_ROZEN TANGERINE SOUFFLÉ

_8 tangerines_
_6 eggs, separated_
_juice of 1 lemon_
_6 oz/175 g sugar_
_³/₄ pint/450 ml double cream_

Grate the zest from 4 of the tangerines and squeeze the juice from all of them. Whisk the zest and juice with the egg yolks, lemon juice and sugar until pale and creamy, then heat gently until the mixture thickens. Do not allow it to boil. Let it cool, then add the lightly whipped cream and finally the stiffly whisked egg whites. Pour into a 1³/₄ pint/1 litre soufflé dish or individual soufflé dishes and freeze for 2–4 hours, depending on the size.

# _V_ANILLA ICE CREAM

_³/₄ pint/450 ml single cream_
_a vanilla pod_
_4 egg yolks_
_5 oz/150 g caster sugar_
_¹/₄ pint/150 ml_
_double cream_

Put the single cream and the vanilla pod – slit lengthways – into a heavy pan and bring slowly to the boil. Remove from the heat and leave to infuse for 15 minutes. Take out the vanilla pod (wash and dry it and keep for further use). Beat the egg yolks and sugar together until thick and pale. Gently reheat the cream and beat a little of it into the egg yolks. Pour the egg mixture into the cream and return the pan to a low heat. Stir until the custard is thick enough to coat the back of a spoon, but do not let it boil. Leave to cool. Whip the double cream lightly and fold it into the custard. Freeze.

# CHOCOLATE ICE CREAM

6 egg yolks
4 oz/125 g vanilla sugar°
3/4 pint/450 ml single cream
6 oz/175 g bitter chocolate
1/4 pint/150 ml double cream

Beat the egg yolks and vanilla sugar until pale and thick. Heat the single cream, pour a little of it onto the egg yolks, then add the egg mixture to the cream. Put the pan back on a low heat and stir until the custard is thick enough to coat the back of a spoon. Leave to cool.

Melt the chocolate in a bowl over a pan of simmering water and stir it into the custard. Whip the double cream lightly, fold it into the mixture and freeze.

°Vanilla sugar is made by keeping a vanilla pod in a jar of sugar, and topping up the sugar as you use it.

# CHOCOLATE AND CHESTNUT PARFAIT

4 fl oz/125 ml syrup (p.25)
4 oz/125 g bitter chocolate
a pinch of ground cloves
3 egg yolks
4 tablespoons chestnut purée
3 marrons glacés, chopped
1/2 pint/300 ml double cream

Heat the syrup gently, almost to boiling point. Melt the chocolate over hot water and stir it into the hot syrup. Stir in the ground cloves. Whisk the egg yolks briskly and pour the chocolate syrup onto them, whisking as you do so. Leave the mixture to cool when it is well blended. Now stir in the chestnut purée, a little at a time, and then the marrons glacés. Whip the cream and fold it in, and freeze.

# CAPPUCCINO ICE CREAM

*½ pint/300 ml single cream*
*3 egg yolks*
*6 oz/175 g caster sugar*
*2 tablespoons strong coffee powder*
*1 teaspoon cocoa*
*1 teaspoon ground cinnamon*
*½ pint/300 ml double cream*

Heat the single cream slowly to boiling point. Beat the egg yolks and sugar until pale and thick, then stir in the coffee, cocoa and cinnamon. Pour on a little of the boiling cream, whisk briskly, then pour the mixture into the cream and heat gently until the custard thickens. Do not let it boil. Leave to cool. Whip the double cream and fold it in, then freeze.

### Variation
Use ½ teaspoon ground cardamom seed instead of the cinnamon.

# MAPLE PECAN ICE CREAM

*8 fl oz/250 ml maple syrup*
*3 egg yolks*
*¾ pint/450 ml double cream*
*4 oz/125 g pecan nuts, chopped*

Heat the maple syrup gently; do not let it boil. Beat the egg yolks and pour on the syrup, whisking briskly until well blended. Leave to cool. Whip the cream and fold it in with the nuts. Freeze.

# HONEY AND WALNUT ICE CREAM

*¹/₂ pint/300 ml milk*
*3 oz/75 g walnuts, chopped coarsely*
*4 oz/125 g honey*
*3 egg yolks*
*2 tablespoons brandy (optional)*
*¹/₄ pint/150 ml double cream*

Bring the milk to the boil, remove the pan from the heat, add the walnuts and leave to infuse for 10 minutes. Heat the honey almost to boiling point. Whisk the egg yolks and pour on the honey, whisking all the time. Beat for 3–4 minutes, until the yolks and honey are well blended. Transfer the mixture to a pan, pour in the milk and walnuts and stir over low heat until the mixture starts to thicken. Do not let it boil. Remove from the heat, cool and then stir in the brandy (if using) and the double cream, lightly whipped. Freeze.

# SINGAPORE ICE CREAM

This recipe is based on one from the *Alice B. Toklas Cook Book*, 1954.

*³/₄ pint/450 ml single cream*
*a vanilla pod*
*6 oz/175 g caster sugar*
*6 egg yolks*
*4 oz/125 g preserved ginger*
*2 oz/50 g walnuts, chopped*
*seeds of 2 cardamoms, ground*
*2 tablespoons whisky (optional)*
*¹/₄ pint/150 ml double cream*

Bring the single cream and vanilla pod to boiling point, then leave to infuse for about 15 minutes. Beat together the sugar and egg yolks until pale yellow. Remove the vanilla pod, wash and dry it and keep for further use. Reheat the cream gently, whisk it into the eggs and then return the mixture to the pan and cook gently until the custard thickens. Leave it to cool. Drain the ginger from its syrup and chop it. Stir it into the custard with the walnuts and cardamom and then the whisky. Whip the double cream and fold it in, then freeze the mixture.

# PRUNE AND ARMAGNAC
## ICE CREAM

*4 fl oz / 125 ml syrup (p.25)*
*3 fl oz / 75 ml armagnac*
*8 oz / 250 g prunes, stoned*
*4 egg yolks*
*4 oz / 125 g caster sugar*
*3/4 pint / 450 ml milk*
*1/4 pint / 150 ml double cream*

Bring the syrup and armagnac
to the boil slowly, then add the
prunes, remove the pan from the
heat, cover it and leave to stand
for an hour. Purée the mixture
and put it aside. Beat the egg
yolks and sugar together until
pale and thick. Heat the milk
and pour it onto the eggs,
whisking steadily. Return the
mixture to the pan and cook
until it is thick enough to coat
the back of a spoon, but
do not let it boil. Leave
to cool. Stir the prune purée
into the custard, fold in
the lightly whipped
cream and freeze.

## COINTREAU ICE CREAM

*vanilla ice cream (p.31)*
*4 oz / 125 g diced crystallized*
*orange peel*
*1/4 teaspoon ground cloves*
*2 fl oz / 50 ml cointreau*

Add the orange peel, cloves and
cointreau to the ice cream just
before freezing.

# PISTACHIO ICE CREAM

*4 oz/125 g pistachios*
*1 oz/25 g almonds, blanched*
*7 oz/200 g sugar*
*1 pint/600 ml milk*
*6 egg yolks*
*¼ pint/150 ml double cream*
*2 tablespoons kirsch*

Grind the nuts with half the sugar – if you use a food processor take care not to let them become oily. Put the nuts and milk into a pan and bring slowly to the boil, stirring occasionally. Remove the pan from the heat, cover it and leave to infuse for 30 minutes. Whisk the egg yolks with the rest of the sugar until thick and pale. Sieve the milk and nut mixture, pushing well through the sieve to extract all the liquid. Bring the milk to the boil again, whisk a little into the egg yolks, then pour the eggs into the pan and put it on a low heat. Stir constantly until the mixture thickens, then leave it to cool. Whip the cream lightly and fold it in with the kirsch. Freeze.

# MRS BEETON'S ICED PUDDING

The recipe is adapted from one in Mrs Beeton's *Household Management*, 1861.

*6 oz/175 g ground almonds*
*6 oz/175 g sugar*
*4 eggs*
*1/2 pint/300 ml single cream*
*1/4 pint/150 ml double cream*

Beat together the almonds, sugar and eggs. Add the single cream and heat gently until the mixture thickens, but do not let it boil. Leave to cool. Whisk the double cream lightly and fold it into the mixture, then freeze.

Mrs Beeton recommends serving the pudding with a compote of fruit; a lightly sweetened purée of raspberries or strawberries makes a good accompaniment. A handful of toasted flaked almonds can be sprinkled over the ice cream.

# QUINCE AND PEAR ICE CREAM

This recipe is based on Jane Grigson's apple and quince ice cream in *Good Things*, 1971.

*2 quinces*
*2 large pears*
*1 oz/25 g butter*
*2 tablespoons water*
*2–4 tablespoons sugar*
*2 eggs, separated*
*1/2 pint/300 ml double cream*
*2 tablespoons eau de vie de poire*

Wash and chop the fruit and cook it until soft in the butter and water with 2 tablespoons of the sugar. Add more sugar if necessary. Purée the fruit through a sieve and stir in the egg yolks. Heat gently for a few minutes until the purée thickens, but make sure it does not boil. Whip the cream until stiff and fold it in with the eau de vie and beaten egg whites. Freeze in an ice cream machine.

If you are freezing the ice cream in trays, add the beaten egg whites after the initial freezing, as if making a sorbet (p.28).

# CINNAMON ICE CREAM

*¹/₂ pint/300 ml single cream*
*5 oz/150 g soft brown sugar*
*2 teaspoons cinnamon*
*4 egg yolks*
*¹/₂ pint/300 ml double cream*

Bring the single cream slowly to the boil with the sugar and cinnamon. Whisk the egg yolks and pour the cream over them, still whisking steadily. Return the mixture to the pan and stir over low heat until it thickens to a custard. Do not let it boil. Whip the double cream lightly and fold it in. Freeze.

# BROWN BREAD ICE CREAM

*³/₄ pint/450 ml double cream*
*4 oz/125 g sugar*
*4 oz/125 g coarse wholemeal breadcrumbs*

Whisk the cream with half of the sugar until it starts to thicken, then freeze the mixture in a tray until the sides and bottom are firm.

Put the breadcrumbs on a baking sheet, sprinkle over the remaining sugar and toast them in a hot oven, 220°C/425°F/gas 7. Leave to cool. Turn the cream out into a chilled bowl, beat it for a minute or two, then stir in the breadcrumb and sugar mixture. Return to the freezer and leave until set.

# FROZEN STRAWBERRY YOGURT

*1 lb/500 g strawberries*
*2 tablespoons kirsch*
*½ pint/300 ml plain yogurt*
*4–5 tablespoons honey*
*2 egg whites*

Purée the strawberries with the kirsch, then mix in the yogurt and honey. Whisk the egg whites and fold them in. Freeze.

### Variations

Use raspberries and cassis or eau de vie de framboise instead of the strawberries and kirsch. Sieve the purée to get rid of the pips before mixing in the yogurt.

Use sliced, stoned apricots and cognac or apricot brandy.

# STRAWBERRY ICE CREAM

Purée *1 lb/500 g strawberries* with *6–8 oz/175–250 g caster sugar.* Add *2 tablespoons lemon juice, ½ pint/ 300 ml double cream* and freeze.

# INDEX

# ACKNOWLEDGEMENTS

*The publishers
would like to thank
the following*

· TYPESETTING ·
TRADESPOOLS LTD
FROME

PHOTOGRAPHIC
· ASSISTANCE ·
JONATHAN BUCKLEY

JACKET
PHOTOGRAPHY ·
DAVE KING

· ILLUSTRATOR ·
JANE THOMSON

· REPRODUCTION
COLOURSCAN
SINGAPORE

PAGE **25,30** MARY EVANS PICTURE LIBRARY, LONDON

GWEN EDMONDS FOR ADDITIONAL HELP
ELINOR BREMAN, SASHA BREMAN AND JUNE KING FOR PREPARING FOOD

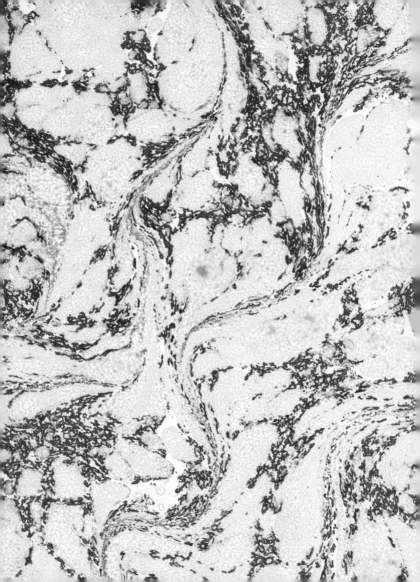